SOULS OF RHYTHM

RHYTHM GUPTA

"For those who seek solace in stanzas

guiding you through life's intricate maze.

the restless minds that rhyme,

A symphony of space and time

May these words kindle the flame within

With each word, may your spirits begin."

Contents

YOU DESERVE IT!

THE BRAVE SURVIVORS

TRUST THE ALMIGHTY

THE FOCUS

Acceptance

Pause

REALITY

THE LITTLE THINGS MATTER

HAVE FAITH

Foreword

In the hushed chambers of the heart, where words flutter like restless birds seeking flight, poetry finds its home. It is within this sacred space that the poet's pen becomes a conduit for emotion, weaving threads of thought into intricate tapestries of verse.

Poetry, with its ability to distill the complexities of existence into succinct expressions, serves as both mirror and muse, reflecting our deepest truths and inspiring new perspectives.

Within these pages, you will encounter a kaleidoscope of emotions, each poem a brushstroke on the canvas of the human experience.

With an open heart and a curious mind, embark upon this odyssey of verse. For within these lines lies the power to awaken, to inspire, and to illuminate.

Preface

Life, with all its twists and turns, is a tapestry woven from moments both profound and mundane. In this collection of poetry, I have endeavored to capture the essence of this intricate tapestry, exploring the myriad facets of existence through the lens of verse.

As you journey through these pages, you will encounter reflections of love's embrace, echoes of grief's lament, and whispers of hope's resilience. Each poem is a snapshot frozen in time, a glimpse into the depths of the human experience.

But beyond mere observation, poetry invites us to engage, to participate in a dialogue with the poet and with ourselves. It beckons us to explore the depths of our own souls, to confront our truths, and to embrace our vulnerabilities.

So let us embark together, dear reader, on this voyage of discovery, as we navigate the ever-changing currents of existence, guided by the compass of poetry. For in the end, it is not the destination that matters, but the moments we share along the way.

-RHYTIIM GUPTA-

Acknowledgements

I am profoundly grateful to everyone who has contributed to the creation of this poetry collection, directly or indirectly. Writing is often a solitary endeavor, but the support and encouragement of others have been invaluable along this journey.

First and foremost, I would like to express my deepest appreciation to MY PARENTS for their unwavering love and support. Their belief in me and my passion for poetry has been a constant source of inspiration.

I extend my heartfelt thanks to my friends, whose feedback and encouragement have helped shape this collection into its final form. Your insights and enthusiasm have been a driving force behind my creative process.

I am indebted to my mentors,MRS.SHIVANI GUPTA,MRS.SHADWAL ANSARI AND MR.SALMAN KHURRAM. Your wisdom and expertise have been instrumental in honing my craft and refining my voice as a poet.

Special thanks to Notionpress for believing in this project and for their dedication to bringing it to fruition. Your professionalism and enthusiasm for literature are truly commendable.

Lastly, I would like to express my gratitude to the readers who have embraced my poetry with open hearts and minds. Your support means the world to me, and I hope that my words resonate with you in meaningful ways.

Thank you, from the bottom of my heart.

Sincerely,

Rhythm gupta.

Prologue

In the quiet depths of the mind's recesses,

There lies a realm where words caress

Within these pages, secrets untold

each stanza a melod,a memory hold

Lies a journey through the soul's embrace,

Weaves tales of love, of loss, of grace.

Where dreams are spun and shadows fade,

Where every word is a serenade.

1. Family

The day I was born
The people who always led me to the throne
Always kept me as their love
They were none other than my family beloved
Grandma, who told me stories
Carried on the legacy of glories
Dad, who treated me as a little one
Give all his strength, so I can have some fun
Mum who never got both of my rants
Aunt and uncle, who appreciated on my achievements
All I know, I have to make them proud
And never let their heads bent
Brothers who are pillars of my life
Sweep all their love for me to dive
Sister, who always need me feel best
They are the confetti to my fest
The most love people of my life
They are the reasons, my life survives .

YOU DESERVE IT!

I hope you are experiencing something today that reminds you that you are on right track. I hope you know that your hard work is worth acknowledging. Even when you haven't achieved anything that you set out to accomplish. I hope you give yourself the credit you deserve.

2. Grandfather (I wish you were here)

Oh heaven! How I wish he was here
Urge to get showered with love and care
How i always craved for my grandfather
How I listened carefully when stories about you were told by
father
I wish you could hold me,see me grow
How much i desperately miss you,wish you could know
The sky and clouds reminds me of you
I know if you were here,you would be the only one to whom I
glued
The way i remember you when I see my friends with their
grandfather
I wish you were so much farther
I know you are seeing me up from heaven
Times when I remember you all week with days of seven
Grandpa, what blessings you gave us as our fathers
Fulfilling their responsibilities is the only thing that matters
Grandma, telling stories about your struggle
How we observe her face when flashbacks of her memories about
you dribble

Oh! How i wish you could see how i fright on stormy nights
Wishing you were here to hold me tight
I hope you are happy up there, blessing us all
Proud seeing us together with all
Now i realise you are so rare
Oh! Grandpa i wish you were here.

THE BRAVE SURVIVORS

perhaps

you were made

for this moment

to walk

through blazing fire

and comeforth

as gold.

3. Neet aspirants

The neet aspirant life I'm living
Another day with hurdles filling
Struggling with chemistry and physics
Writing everything in lyrics
Painkillers are the part of the day
how I feel like giving up everytime I say
peer pressure of being successful
going to and fro from coaching and school
Nights are my best friends
Skipping out on every trends
I know this isn't easy
But don't be so cosy
If it was at such ease everyone could do it
You're the main character just don't stop and sit
Remember you've goals to reach
Learn from everything that teach
Future holds surgeries, blood and needles
Be the limelight that kindles
Reminder you've to be a doctor
You're your own Rockstar
Parents smiling and standing proud
getting cheers all the way through the crowd

Two years of suffering and sacrifices
Everything will be good after numerous practices
Here I stand high and strong
we know the journey is long
Shoutout to all the motivating poster
All my best wishes to future doctors

TRUST THE ALMIGHTY

YOU MAY NOT SEE IT NOW BUT GOD WILL NEVER PUT YOU IN A SEASON IF HE DIDN'T HAVE A HARVEST READY FOR YOU IN THE NEXT

4. The Mentors

The spice to the life

The blade to the knife

Way they are incomplete without each other

That's the way we're incomplete without our teachers

The day shouldn't be specific to celebrate them

Cause they are the gems

Cones to the ice cream

The way our teachers gives us wings to dream

From holding our fingers and making us write

To explaining us how things in life will go right

From making us learn the English alphabets

To giving us all the huge responsibility to organise the comfests

From becoming our second guardians on first day of school

To handling us on farewell when our eyes water as a pool

That's how my memory will forever reverse

They are relief to our Pain like painkillers

English being changed upside down

Tenses and pronouns were in syllabus were years ago

From studying mass and weight in physics

Never knew how entered the principle of archimedes

Chemistry filled with elements name

Upgraded itself up with all organic IUPAC name

Biology full of plants and animal types
Never noticed how much anatomy hypes
The last pen down is to the teacher who make this fun
Make all the things done at once
The spice to life
The blade to knife
That's how I'm thankful to them all my life.

THE FOCUS

BE DISCIPLINED! THERE IS NO EASY WAY. THERE ARE ONLY LATE NIGHTS,HARDWORK,EARLY MORNINGS,EMPTY POCKETS AND NO FRIENDS.

ONLY YOU,YOUR BELIEF AND GOD.<3

5. The Night of Odds

Crashing down of stress
Coming alongwith distress
Even the evens convert to odds
Loyals into frauds
Ours into illegitimate
Without any options left alternate
Bearing of the survival
Almost a proper fullstop on an ongoing fable
That's how the worlds comes crashing down
With shades of black and brown
Heads and brains messed up
Even the birds don't chirp
Hues of sorrows around
With almost a person in thoughts drowned
Thinking power clashes even at a point Without a mediator
without a joint
Almost of a wrong timings
With sorrow blinding
An alone confused in a crowd
That's how it brings the night of odd.
ReplyForward
Add reaction

acceptance

YOU DO NOT HAVE IT TODAY BECAUSE YOU DID NOT WORK HARD FOR IT YESTERDAY.

ITS AS SIMPLE AS THAT.

Chapter6

In the midst of a busy life
When in crowds, the people thrive
A person wanders in cloud of thoughts
Never knew the time he fought
Doing things altogether
When task pile up and gather
Management is all needed
A mindful of stress needed
Messed up person, messed up brain
When clouds of tension rain
As the time slips out of hand
As smooth as sand.
The chaos of day and night
Doesn't make anyone feel alright
Somethings are as clear as crystal
Everything as the time gets distal.

pause

<u>Practice the pause . A person who pauses before reacting is a powerful person. when you stop reacting to people disrespect it ruins their power over you.</u>

7. COMPANIONS

The sparks to the life
My most favourite tribe
Humans making life simple
Like stars in the sky twinkle
Blessings on us
The best people to have faith and trust
Hand-in-hand together
Calm silence in a stormy thunder
Helping one another in need
Without a pinch of lie and greed
Lighting in the darkness
Hanging out with them is the best .
In the midst of a busy life
They are the best peace
On a sunny day, they are the breeze
Friendship, a blessing on earth
A pure boon since birth.

REALITY

Action speak in the end

If someone does not want you

They won't even care if you

Rip your heart out

Keep trying lifetime <3

8. SHOWERED BLISS

The blessings almost under rated
Though sometimes outdated
The live without medicines to live
With Love of mom and dad, we survive
Being able to walk without crutches
When a life of disabled ditches
Ability to breathe natural air
A life without someone's under care
Hands of grandparents on our heads
A bond's unbreakable thread
Love and presence of sibling
Heart, full of love filling
A life full of smiles
When for others, tension piles
I got to pray to
I'm always grateful for these blessings though.

THE LITTLE THINGS
MATTER

**Your diet is not only what you eat . It's what you watch, what you listen, what you read, the people who hang around with,Be mindful of the things you put into your body, emotionally, spiritually, and physically.**

9. FROSTY DAYS

In midst of my summers and springs
A season so cold and chilly swings
The foggy mornings, the sights
Dew drops on window at nights
Soups and coffee. The saviours.
When temperature reaches to 0°C nearer
The wait to look up and see the sun
With warm, the bonfire burns
A cosy winter blanket and quilt
Feeling to stay under covers build
Places with snowfalls and snowflakes
Time of year when Christmas cake gets baked
Glaciers and rivers turns frozen
with everyone's blurry and foggy vision
That's how the subcontinental winds enter
And blesses us with a chilly and frosty winters.

HAVE FAITH

God is still writing your story. Stop trying to steal the pen. Trust the author<3

10. DECLINING OF THE GOLDEN PHASE

A wave of enthusiasm
Life is perfect with its light dim
12th class, a new phase
An unfolding of a new daze
A full stop to the school life
The path of life is yet to drive
A farewell , tears to the journey
A challenge of academics to many
Boards class this year
Calm and put on the beautiful smile, you wear
Lot of stress and tension
Streams, we chose not forgetting to mention
World revolving around NCERT's
Coaching have now been our besties
The aim for hard work to gather name, and fame
It's the way to win this competition game.

Every Second Happens For A Reason

"If you prayed for something, celebrate it with him.
Return the glory to where it belongs.